Going Inside

ALSO BY RAY LEONARDINI

Finding God Within
Contemplative Prayer for Prisoners

"I only wish I had this guidance and advice when I was a jail chaplain for fourteen years. You do not need to fly by the seat of your pants anymore! When you have access to a man as patient and experienced as Ray Leonardini, you would be wise to let him guide you—in one of the least supported and yet most needed ministries of Christianity."

—**Fr. Richard Rohr, O.F.M.**, Center for Action and Contemplation; author, *Breathing under Water*

Going Inside

Learning to Teach Contemplative Prayer to the Imprisoned

RAY LEONARDINI

Prison Contemplative Fellowship

Foreword by THOMAS KEATING

Lantern Books ● *New York*
A Division of Booklight Inc.

2016
Lantern Books
128 Second Place
Brooklyn, NY 11231
www.lanternbooks.com

Printed in the United States of America

For additional copies, free to prisoners, please write to: Prison
Contemplative Fellowship, P.O. Box 1086, Folsom, CA 95763-1086,
USPCF.org, email: office@USPCF.org.

Library of Congress Cataloging-in-Publication Data

Names: Leonardini, Ray, author.
Title: Going inside : learning to teach contemplative
prayer to the imprisoned / Ray Leonardini, Prison
Contemplative Fellowship ; foreword by Thomas Keating.
Description: New York City : Lantern Books, 2016. |
Includes bibliographical references and index.
Identifiers: LCCN 2016032929 (print) | LCCN
2016033543 (ebook) | ISBN 9781590565490 (pbk. : alk.
paper) | ISBN 9781590565506 ()
Subjects: LCSH: Prisoners—Religious life—Study
and teaching. | Contemplation—Study and teaching. |
Prayer—Christianity—Study and teaching.
Classification: LCC BV4595 .L46 2016 (print) | LCC
BV4595 (ebook) | DDC 259/.5—dc23
LC record available at https://lccn.loc.gov/2016032929

Prison Contemplative Fellowship is a community of prisoners, former prisoners, their families, chaplains, and volunteers who practice a form of Christian silent prayer called centering prayer. It is a fellowship that recognizes our individuality and celebrates our unique relationship with the Divine.

The symbol of the Cross, adapted for prisoners, points to the key to our freedom. We acknowledge that it is through the mysterious transformation of our suffering in centering prayer that brings the vital change we deeply desire.

Contents

A Hedge on Discouragement
"I Can't Teach the Spiritual Journey"
Practical Realities of Going into a Prison

About the Author
Also by Lantern Books
About the Publisher

Foreword
Thomas Keating

What does visiting those in prison do for them? Actually, they are probably asking themselves why you came. You don't have to say anything besides ordinary ways of greeting anyone such as, "How are you today?" Or simply, "Hello." It is your presence that touches them. Since they are not your friends or relatives, why would you give them time you could be spending with those you love or in entertaining yourself?

Your presence is bearing witness to their basic goodness. This is what God does whenever he reveals his mercy. In visiting the imprisoned, you are manifesting the mercy of God to them just by being there. You are sharing with them the divine mercy that you have received and that they desperately need.

Your visit may give a boost to prisoners who are depressed and self-hating because of their past, to realize and accept their basic goodness. It is only a short step further for them to experience God's forgiveness and to recover the deep self-respect that can only come from the realization of being loved. This will enable them to forgive themselves.

If in addition to just being there you offer an explanation of the centering prayer method, some will start practicing it every day in their cell. They will need to be sustained by more information and by sharing their experiences with each other.

Pray and meditate with them when you visit. After a while, you yourself will be greatly enriched, as you watch them changing before your eyes.

Offer centering prayer as a gift. There is no obligation on their part to practice it and please avoid anything like proselytizing. Thus, a relationship of friendship will build up and allow the Spirit of God to work freely both in you and in them, creating a community of love that will surpass the spiritual level of most of the people who are not in prison.

I invite you to read this little book describing the experiences of prisoners doing centering prayer. If you feel inspired to join them, you will have God's eternal gratitude.

Preface

Susan Komis

Director, Contemplative Outreach, Ltd.

In the fall of 2014, Ray Leonardini invited me to accompany him to a class at Folsom Prison that he offers to inmates. Ray has been volunteering weekly for the past eight years at Folsom, teaching inmates about contemplative spirituality and introducing them to a practice of centering prayer. I was asked to observe what he is offering to the inmates who voluntarily attend.

Ray was meeting with two different groups of Folsom inmates. One met on Monday evenings with nearly 40 inmates. The other group met on Thursday mornings and a dozen or so inmates came. I attended as guest and observer. My experience of those meetings is etched in my memory.

We sit in a circle with volunteers and inmates alike. They settle in their chairs and move into a 20-minute period of silence. Silence is a luxury that they cannot find in their cellblocks. Following this time of silent prayer, Ray offers informative teachings intended to inspire and open minds and hearts; he leads a discussion where inmates share their stories, often tinged with sorrow and despair, and in contrast, their hopes and dreams for the future. Some of the men share, while others listen.

I am both an observer and listener. I am praying interiorly for a magic wand that an invisible someone will wave around the circle with the hope that, miraculously, all present will be transformed and life here at Folsom will be but a dim memory or bad dream. No magic wand appears.

The men in the groups are thoroughly engaged in the group process. I wonder what inner prompting has brought them to this gathering. I glance around the circle and memorize the names of the inmates. I mentally recall the faces in the circle and write their names on a scrap of paper on the flight returning home. I carry that paper with me for months after visiting Folsom with Ray, taking the paper out occasionally and recalling each person . . . the faces of Harold, Lawrence, Jimmy, and Angel come to mind.

A teenager sits next to me on the plane. Ironically, he tells me he has just been released from juvenile detention where he has been incarcerated for two years. He is traveling to the city where I reside to live with his older sister. His mother is in prison. He shows me the list of goals that he made before his release and hopes to achieve in this new environment. Perhaps there *is* a magic wand. It is winter and he has no coat. I add his name to my recall list.

I was privileged to visit Folsom again with Ray in 2015. He has begun to form other volunteers who feel a call to serve in prisons and share centering prayer with inmates in local prison facilities and in facilities across the country. It is difficult to gain entrance in the prison system in the state where I live, but I am inspired to try again to offer my service as a volunteer.

Introduction

This extended essay is written for prison chaplains and volunteers who are beginning a practice of centering prayer in prisons and jails. It assumes familiarity with *Finding God Within: Contemplative Prayer for Prisoners* (Lantern Books, 2016).

The purpose of *Going Inside* is to function as a guidebook, pointing out things to recognize along the way. The first part describes a spirituality of the incarcerated: how the life of the Spirit emerges as we get to know men and women who are spending years of their lives in prison. In the second part, the essay addresses the normal apprehension we experience when we decide to go into a prison or jail. It provides practical suggestions for what to actually do in a group. Finally, it offers prisoners' testimonies of appreciation on the value of volunteers joining them in contemplative prayer.

It is my hope that reading this and experiencing the wonder of participating in contemplative prayer in a prison or jail will give prison chaplains and volunteers a sense of what a *privilege* it is to pray with the incarcerated, and what a source of grace.

Then I heard the voice of the Lord saying, "Whom shall I send, and who will go for us?" And I said, "Here am I; send me!"—Isaiah 6:8

Part 1

A Spirituality of the Incarcerated

I am here to share your situation and to make it my own. I have come so that we can pray together and offer our God everything that causes us pain, but also everything that gives us hope, so that we can receive from him the power of the resurrection. Jesus comes to meet us, so that he can restore our dignity as children of God. He wants us to keep walking along the paths of life, to realize that we have a mission, and that confinement is not the same thing as exclusion.
—**Pope Francis** *to inmates at Curran-Frombold Correctional Facility, Philadelphia, September 27, 2015*

Prisoners are a perfect fit for contemplative prayer. We might think that such prayer is reserved for hidden-away monks, not for ordinary people, and most certainly not for the unschooled. For centuries, it was not taught to lay people. The free-to-all gift of God stayed in monasteries for the most part. It remained a somewhat hidden prayer practice.

Meditation first emerged in California prisons as Buddhist Insight Meditation. This practice is generally better known in prisons than contemplative prayer. Part of its success in the pluralistic religious environment of prisons is that it is not specifically described as prayer and makes no formal mention of prayer as a relationship with God. The fact that Christianity also has a long, rich tradition of meditation is a novel, heretofore-unknown idea for many, including some Christian prison chaplains.

It was simply beyond the spiritual imagination of those who taught us to pray that this contemplative prayer practice could be experienced by those considered "unworthy" in our society. How things have changed! If you are reading this monograph you know of the amazing rise of contemplative meditation practices like centering prayer in prisons and jails throughout our country. Remarkable things are happening for prisoners and for those who facilitate this form of prayer in prisons. Let me try to explain why this is so.

Crossing Over[*]

I started practicing centering prayer with prisoners at Folsom Prison in late 2008. At the time, I was stumbling around looking for a centering prayer group in which I could feel welcomed and challenged. On my way to Folsom for the first time I wondered about my ability to connect with prisoners, whether I could be honest with them about my own confusion, and if my latent fear for my own security would undermine my ability to be present to them. I asked myself: *Am I this desperate to find a group that I need to pray with a captive audience?*

In the ensuing years, facilitating two prayer groups a week at Folsom, I discovered a hidden treasure of inestimable value. The treasure was not simply hidden from unsuspecting prisoners; it was hidden from me! The more I participated in centering prayer with prisoners, the more I recognized that I was also changing. I watched as prisoners, as they themselves testify, re-envisioned their relationship with God. They moved from a view of God and themselves built on shame and guilt to one envisioning God as the Father of the Prodigal Son, freely and unconditionally

[*] I would like to thank Sister Suzanne Jabrow for the term "crossing over."

expressing love for prisoners. It usually started by prisoners telling me they had discovered a subtle ability to cut themselves some slack. They realized, seemingly quite naturally, that they were neither the worst person in the world nor the best. They could feel, ever so softly, that God could indeed love them.

The more I tried to teach this "God Within," and the more I heard prisoners' comments about changes in their inner life, the more I found myself *crossing over* into some new gravitational field of spirituality. In this spirituality, the narrative uses a uniquely Christian story, that of Jesus of Nazareth. But this is the Jesus *before* Christianity. In particular, this Jesus is the person who had a significant "opening" at his baptism and spent the rest of his life, and death, coming to terms with its ramifications.

In this "spirituality of the incarcerated," Jesus' companionship with the marginalized was much more than a compassionate acceptance of those who were "unclean" and ostracized by the religious establishment at the time. It was, in fact, the place where he found his community of meaning and perspective. It was the place where he could actually grasp the goodness and unconditional love of the Ultimate Mystery he called *Father* in the presence of "the least of these." His experience of the Father determined how he saw the marginalized. His experience of the marginalized gave him greater awareness of the love of the Father.

After a while, I felt the earth beneath me shift. Along with prisoners, I too was re-envisioning the foundation stones of my own spirituality. The idea of doing "good works" for the disadvantaged now seemed off-point. Now I had to acknowledge that prisoners' reflection of the love of the Father was changing my basic notions of how God works in the world. It was as though prisoners were also teaching me, although they had no idea that this was going on. Before my own eyes I could see why the marginalized and discarded were truly God's "favorites." Nor was I then moved to the periphery by their new status. We were all experiencing the unbounded largesse of God.

> *Before my own eyes I could see why the marginalized and discarded were truly God's "favorites." Nor was I then moved to the periphery by their new status. We were all experiencing the unbounded largesse of God.*

As I passed through the gates and cellblocks to get to the chapel, I would have chance encounters with various members of our group. In their own way, ever so briefly, they would tell me what was really going on in their lives. This became the material that I would mull over between visits and try to put into words for the next class. Eventually, I expanded my prepared texts of prayer principles and spiritual-journey pointers with the actual experiences of group members. It was more authentic to make explicit the inner experience of the prisoners.

My inner experience became fair game to the prisoners. This became abundantly clear to me recently. Just before I came into the prison one Monday night I had been on the phone with the father of one of the prisoners who had been in our group and who had paroled the year before. I learned that this parolee had relapsed, broken the law to finance his addiction, and would be going back to prison. The news had a tremendous emotional impact on me. Apparently my frame of mind was so obvious that two of our prison group members asked me: "OK, you don't have to tell us, but there is something serious going on for you. What's up?" The sharing in the group creates this reciprocal vulnerability.

Using Gospel Stories

As I "crossed over" into contemplative practices with prisoners, I found gospel stories helped prisoners decipher their experiences, irrespective of their religion or Bible knowledge. These gospel parables and stories unveiled the inner life of Jesus in a way that *allowed prisoners to map their own contemplative experiences.* Prisoners realized that their experiences, just as with Jesus, came from the same *Source* and had the same goal: intimacy with God. Prisoners started to reframe their own contorted life events using the images that Jesus described. I found that I could discuss Jesus as the model of contemplative experience without getting trapped in theological debates or Christian doctrines.

> *I have found this approach of focusing on the life of Jesus before his resurrection (before Christianity) to have the effect of increasing the depth of prisoners' relationship with Christ.*

It is difficult to overestimate the importance of this switch in approaching scripture. When prisoners are freed from a literal interpretation of the Bible, so frequently foisted on them by well-meaning chaplains and volunteers (and other prisoners), a new depth of meaning is opened to them. Jesus is no longer the teacher (and enforcer) of moral strictures. He becomes the bearer of the good news of the Ultimate Mystery's love. Now all of us hang on his every word and deed because this man, Jesus, does in fact have the words of eternal life.

Since those beginnings, I have found this approach of focusing on the life of Jesus before his resurrection (before Christianity) to have the effect of *increasing* the depth of prisoners' relationship with Christ. This makes sound instructional sense because most people find the human person of Jesus to be authentic, real, and irresistible. It is not my explicit goal to bring prisoners to Christ. Prisoners discover this for themselves once the teachings about Jesus they learned in childhood are freed from literal explanations. Jesus becomes the *messenger* of the experience of the Ultimate Mystery.

The message is not limited to Christians. Prisoners see that the parables and stories of Jesus are not simply moral imperatives. They are his personal revealing of his own contemplative experience of his journey to the Father. Jesus' words, parables, and choices become our discernment tools. These tools can be used by prisoners, chaplains, and volunteers alike, in our shared journey into contemplative living. For the first time, we understand that it is the faith *of* Jesus in the Ultimate Mystery he called *Father* that is pivotal in our contemplative journey.

We begin to trust Jesus at a whole new level. As we consent to the presence and action of God Within, we come to realize we are no longer "doing" contemplative prayer, but contemplative prayer is "doing us." This comes on its own. In this respect, we do not make a traditional "act of faith." It is more that we recognize and discover that this trust is flowing inside of us. It is less about will power and more about surrendering to the inner unfolding in our lives. We look to scripture more as the prime articulator of our own wordless experiences of the Divine. We find that there is an entirely new sense of empowerment. As we discover our vulnerability before the Divine, we experience our own uniqueness and goodness. We recognize that our growing sense of compassion is a reflection of the Compassion "present and active" within.

Is Contemplative Spirituality Only for Christians?

I was recently invited to explain our program to all the prison chaplains in a facility that did not have a centering prayer program. In the exchange, I mentioned that centering prayer did not require Christian beliefs. The Jewish chaplain looked at the book *Finding God Within: Contemplative Prayer for Prisoners*, and asked: "If it's not solely for Christians, why is there a section in the book on the Contemplative Jesus?"

I answered by saying that Christianity was my religious orientation; I was born and raised as a Catholic. I said that if I had as great a familiarity with the Buddha, I would be quoting him as well. Clearly, Buddhists had no problem quoting Jesus to emphasize their point. Jesus simply gave me the best expression of engaging the mystery of Ultimate Reality. I said this prayer is not a prayer of separation; it is a prayer to the One God of all.

At that point the imam spoke up and recited his "favorite" Rumi poem:

I looked for God in church and couldn't find him;
I looked for God in the synagogue and couldn't find him;
I looked for God in the mosque and couldn't find him;
I looked for God inside and found him.

All the chaplains affirmed the spirit of Rumi.

The "unmediated" experience of God in contemplative prayer is a primal experience of God. It is prior to words, concepts, theological principles, and denominational explanations. We come to "know" God by this wordless, intimate experience. Our culture and education take over and "explain" what this means in our daily life. My spiritual home is Christianity. My understanding of God's ways with me is handed down from centuries past by people like you and me who reflect on their experiences of the Divine. This is theology. It helps me understand what is happening to me, but the *experience* comes first. It need not be understood as exclusively Christian. This primal experience is the domain of contemplative prayer.

I rely on those theological principles that are consistent with my experience. You are free to choose yours. Contemplative prayer transforms our unique, no-one-in-the-world-like-us experience into a self that reflects the image and likeness of God. This is our emphasis in teaching contemplative prayer. It allows a prisoner to have his or her unique self come out and be recognized.

Discerning the Invitation

This essay is written for the person who asks: *Do I want to teach and facilitate contemplative prayer in a prison or jail?* I have spoken to scores of people around the country who are attracted by the idea of sitting in contemplative prayer with prisoners. Some are currently working as prison chaplains or prayer-group volunteers. Others are considering volunteering. They come to Prison Contemplative Fellowship from various places, but their interest is the same. They experience some type of "draw" but are not sure how to proceed. They know their own personal deficiencies. They are fully aware that many times their personal prayer is anything but remarkable. They see the lack of support from church groups, and they wonder if they can do it on their own. Some have read the book *Finding God Within: Contemplative Prayer for Prisoners*, and they marvel at the prisoners' statements of their experiences. But the task seems daunting. They don't know how to start.

If they are prison chaplains, or currently volunteering, they often don't feel sure of a way to explain the spiritual journey. They say: *Now that I'm in the prison or jail and have started a group, what next? Is there any systematic way to teach the subtleties of the journey?* Some ask: *Do I have the right to uncover long-suppressed trauma for prisoners when I have little background in psychology or counseling?*

These uncharted regions of contemplative spirituality for prisoners can discourage chaplains and volunteers. The prison experience is unlike prayer-group experiences of educated, middle-class white people who are sincerely trying to deepen their devotional life. Prison work is entirely different and often frustrating. In prison we deal, whether we are prepared to or not, with people who have had horrendous personal experiences. Often, we don't know what to say. Often, we are heartbroken at the enormity of the suffering we see plainly in front of us. We wonder if this person is mentally ill or experiencing the work of the Spirit. We question the appropriateness of what we're doing with such fragile souls. Can we, in good faith, teach a receptive meditation practice that will undoubtedly open prisoners to their own unconscious material? Do we have the skill set to do this?

We all need to associate with people facing these same dilemmas. Together, we are a community of privilege. This is not the privilege of middle-class security and economic "blessings." It is the privilege of finding ourselves called to attend to the sufferings of society's discarded, the very people who seem to be God's "favorites." We must support each other.

A Map for the Journey

The handbook *Finding God Within: Contemplative Prayer for Prisoners* was designed and written to give prisoners a map for their contemplative journey. The sections unfold intuitively from the common experiences of prisoners who are attracted to silent meditation and yet have no exposure to recognized traditions of spirituality.

The sections don't follow a logical progression as chapters in a math book might progress. They emerge from three related sources. The first is the Introductory Workshop material developed by Thomas Keating's Contemplative Outreach, particularly the four guidelines for doing centering prayer. This is the basic component for teaching contemplative prayer.

The second source of material is the direct testimony of the prisoners. This is as important a source as the Introductory Workshop materials. Prisoners will tell you what they need, although they usually don't know they are telling you. Before one class, I was waiting in line with a prisoner who had been in a small group with me for about a year. We hadn't spoken alone before. He told me how much he needed the space he gets from doing centering prayer. Then he said, "You know, I have a constant battle going on inside of me. The devil is trying to take me off my path. It's driving me crazy." I heard a desperate and frantic plea as though the prisoner believed he was in a last-ditch effort to save his soul.

As he shared his inner experience with me, I experienced the intensity of his struggle. It literally felt like life and death to him. He was trying his best to unscramble the competing contortions of his life. It reminded me that this *was* a life issue for this man. He couldn't be trying harder. As it turned out that day, this internal experience of mine reiterated the importance of teaching centering prayer as a *receptive* method of meditation. Without repeating the conversation, and violating the prisoner's confidence, I used his disclosure to me to teach the foundational "letting go of *thoughts*" with more depth and intensity.

The prisoner's confession also reminded me that for many prisoners, and for many preachers in prisons, it really *is* the devil trying to take them off their path. Coming at this complicated, literalist view of the devil by placing the battle in the context of a "thought" to be released affords a pedagogical opportunity as well. The members of the group are more inclined to get deeper into their process when they recognize their own struggle in the struggle of another prisoner. Prisoners have no idea how their personal communications to us can effectively provide a basis for important dimensions of our teaching.

The third source of these sections in *Finding God Within* comes from my own prayer practice, no matter how chaotic it appears to be. I've come to accept that much of my material is related to the material that is emerging for prisoners. Which material emerges first I cannot tell; I just know they are connected. This material gives me clues and tips for the next lesson. If I'm experiencing discouragement, some in the group, if not most, are also experiencing discouragement. My willingness to engage this connection, and maybe even talk about it, gives substance to the process. My knowledge of the group guides the depths of the discussion. I have only to look honestly inside to find the next topic, to develop the next lesson.

Finally, in my opinion, there is no doubt that a person cannot, and should not, teach and facilitate contemplative prayer with prisoners if he or she does not have his or her own contemplative prayer practice.

> *In my opinion, there is no doubt that a person cannot, and should not, teach and facilitate contemplative prayer with prisoners if he or she does not have his or her own contemplative prayer practice.*

Through the interaction of these sources, I wrote *Finding God Within* as one way through the intricacies of the spiritual journey. It is not the only way. Each year has opened a different trail through this spiritual terrain. One year, the emphasis was on the way the ubiquitous and invisible experience of shame slays the soul of the person experiencing the shame. The next time through the contemplative material the emphasis may be on the "game-changing" awareness of early childhood trauma. But this critical point must be made: If one is to teach contemplative prayer to prisoners, one must be willing in some way to address the uniqueness of our shared spiritual journey.

Is There a Preferred Group Process?

Whether the prison or jail is a maximum-security facility or some other kind, there are some general, unwritten rules of engagement that operate in every facility. They involve the politics of race and religion. From a racial point of view, prisoners learn that as a general matter they must be careful when talking with a prisoner from another race. In Folsom this is not an absolute prohibition, but an expected norm for interaction. For example, in the yard there is one full basketball court. One half of the court is for African-Americans only, the other for whites and others. One *never* sees a white basketball player on the court set aside for blacks. This rule isn't written anyplace. But everybody understands the rule.

Religious demarcations are more subtle, but just as prevalent. It plays out like this: *My religion, or my religious practice, makes much more sense than yours.* In fact, some prisoners ask directly: "How can you justify your religious beliefs in the first place?" Most inmates think this, and some will talk this way. When inmates come to prison they must disclose their religious preferences. The denominational lines of demarcation are clearly drawn.

Talking and sharing personal experiences, particularly the personal experiences associated with the "unloading of the unconscious," must be viewed in the context of these unwritten rules for prisoners in a contemplative prayer group. This is particularly significant if the prison facility has one chapel that all must share, as is the case at Folsom Prison.

When prisoners leave the yard to come into the chapel for meditation they are making both a political and religious statement for all to see: they are willing to suspend for the next 90 minutes the rules of the yard. This stops some inmates from coming, and discourages others who are not yet able to leave their peer-group comfort zone. By coming into the chapel, no matter their race or religion, the prisoner is consenting to a subtle solidarity with the other inmates who practice contemplative prayer in the group. This creates a social bond that doesn't exist in the yard. There is a newfound freedom of association that can be unusually satisfying. Prisoners find that contemplative prayer moves them toward compassion, justice, and inclusivity. This is an observable way station on their journey toward intimacy with God, a profound personal transformation—the ultimate resting place for contemplatives.

> *In this space we spontaneously recognize that the hysteria of our anger and bitterness is really not getting us anywhere.*

Once I first observed this social dynamic at the beginning of our gatherings, and began to understand its underpinnings, I was all for allowing this new communal fabric to be developed in its own way and its own time. We would

talk first, sometimes about contemplative prayer, sometimes about related topics, then sit in meditation at the end
of the session. Often, we ran out of time and had to cut off
a good discussion to "meditate." Over a period of months,
I came to realize that these early, fruitful discussions were
at the expense of a more serious engagement with the
specifics of the spiritual journey. In other words, while
the conversations that arose when the inmates first came
into the chapel were an opportunity to expand racial and
religious boundaries, they actually compromised a fuller
experience of the depths of contemplation, their spiritual
journey, and a deeper personal exchange.

When I started the gatherings with centering prayer
I found that the discussions after silence were of a deeper
order. The longer it took prisoners to come back to ordinary awareness, the deeper they had gone during their
prayer period. Then I noticed a *substantial* change in the
way the discussion proceeded. The "nonordinary" space of
centering prayer lingered after the prayer. This nonordinary
space is difficult to describe with precision, but its attributes
are not those of our ordinary, walking-around experience.
In this nonordinary space we are experiencing a different
sense of ourselves; we seem to be underneath our usual
narratives and judgments. It is not an uncomfortable, scary
spot of being high or in any way out of control. In this space
we spontaneously recognize that the hysteria of our anger
and bitterness is really not getting us anywhere. Here, we are
more capable of releasing our worn-out resentments and
group memories. Prisoners now brought greater presence
to the discussion after prayer. They became more willing to
engage on a deeper level.

Now group members come from various cellblocks over a period of 20 to 30 minutes and file into the chapel. This is a time to meet and greet. Once the group is complete, we begin the movement to centering prayer. Some brief words reminding the inmates of the seriousness of the prayer they are about to enter set the stage for them to close their eyes: a statement of trust in the security of the group. I always use a brief bit of music for a last push into the deep. Time and again in evaluations, prisoners at Folsom, but not all prisons, unanimously affirm the value of this sacred music. (I use cuts from various artists. The five-volume CD set of *Sacred Treasures* is a good source.) At the end of the meditation, silence for a short period can be a really helpful lead-in to the discussion for the night.

Presenting a Topic

All of us miss large portions of any spoken presentation. This is particularly true when the presentation unearths challenging personal material. I assume that my listeners get about 50 percent of the presentation on the first bounce. It helps me to appreciate this when I discover that I did not understand a certain topic at all until I tried to teach it. We carefully tutor first-time attendees by giving them a copy of *Finding God Within* and a short explanation of what they can expect during the meeting. In addition, especially when we are exploring a topic in depth, we give inmates a handout that summarizes what we are going to do that night. They can read it ahead of time, listen to the teaching, discuss its meaning or their experience, and read it again when they go back to their cell. We also include carefully selected quotations from wisdom teachers to both reinforce the teaching point of the lesson, and expose them to the best contemplative literature.

Many prisoners are not drawn to read traditional books about spirituality. Such books are culturally and educationally foreign and intimidating. However, when a quote in a handout aptly touches a topic of the discussion, or a particular citation from *Finding God Within* illustrates the point, prisoners are more likely to take the leap and read the book.

The Next Obvious Step

The particular ways in which contemplative prayer informs the daily life of prisoners in a particular facility is unique to the facility and the idiosyncrasies of the group members. In my view, it is a mistake to impose a ready-made, one-size-fits-all syllabus no matter its attractiveness as a ready-to-use guide. It is much more true to the process to rely on the Spirit to guide you to the next topic for the group, through your own process of discernment. The topics in *Finding God Within* are guidelines and suggestions to support your discernment. What is best here is for you, the instructor/facilitator, to go inside your own contemplative experience; test it against the experiences of the group and your own knowledge of the spiritual journey; and find the applicable next obvious step.

Part 2

Starting a Contemplative Prayer Group

Starting a contemplative prayer practice in prison, as a volunteer or chaplain, is like packing your bags for a journey without any sense of destination. Imagine yourself sitting with a group of prisoners. You not only don't know them, they don't know one another. Together, you have very little idea where this group is heading. You are stocked full of contemplative prayer, perhaps centering prayer ideas, books, and resources. You are well aware of your own limitations and have only stereotypical assumptions of the limitations of the prisoners in front of you. Now what do you do?

Starting at the Beginning

The idealistic ideas of creating a contemplative lifestyle in a penitentiary, appropriate and doable as they are, come down to starting at the beginning: *Get to know the prisoners by letting them get to know you, the real you.* This simple principle plays itself out in every lesson that you mutually explore with prisoners. It's not about your downloading all you've learned from your personal contemplative practice. It's more disclosing what you've learned and being willing to go public with it. As importantly, it involves being willing to listen, truly listen to their experience, however seemingly unrelated to the material at hand it may appear to be.

> The contemplative mind should be religion's unique gift to society. It greases the wheels of spiritual evolution.—**Richard Rohr,** *Immortal Diamond,* p. 118

Prisoners are less interested in your ideas and concepts about meditation. They are interested in *who you are*, and why you're coming into the desolate and dreary place they are trying to leave. They are much too respectful of you, and grateful for your coming into the prison, to say this out loud. This is actually good news for you because it prompts you to give up any phony notion that you can teach them something they don't already know. It pushes you in the direction of trying to be honest about your personal attempts at contemplative living.

Recently, at the invitation of a prison chaplain, three of us gave an introduction to contemplative prayer in prison to a members of a prison group called Criminals and Gangmembers Anonymous (CGA) who were considering starting a contemplative prayer weekly group. Two of us were well-schooled in the fundamentals of centering prayer's Introductory Workshop principles. That's what we talked about. The third person in our group was not. She was "just a volunteer" drawn to prison work, willing to overcome her fear. When her turn came to speak, she offered no conceptualization, no experienced insight. She simply talked about her love of centering prayer and how much it changed her life. She spoke honestly of her true motivation to accompany these prisoners in the same journey, not because she knew something they didn't, but because it seemed like the right thing to do. The effect on these CGA members was palpable. Her honesty and humility reached these men in a fashion the two of us could not.

The Difference between Honesty and Openness

The more honest you can be with your attempts at contemplative living, the more attractive the prospect becomes to prisoners actually trying to find a contemplative lifestyle. The attraction is in the nature of the contemplative experience when we hear of a genuine attempt to live on a different level of awareness. It is so unusual we actually want to give it a chance. Your talking about your personal experience with this type of prayer affords an implicit encouragement to prisoners that they can try it as well. Your honesty is attractive. Your willingness to explore with them the rigors of silence is a bonus.

Personal, self-revealing stories are less attractive, particularly stories filled with personal drama. How do you know you've crossed into personal drama in your examples? When you use examples that demonstrate that you are a victim in the situation you describe. Put differently, we enter into drama when we take our slights personally. One of the first experiences of contemplative living that prisoners will talk about is exactly the situation where they realize that they are not the focus of the conflict. Their awareness allows them to see that the correctional officer is not picking on them personally. He's just having "a bad day" and they happen to be the recipient of his anger.

Beginners' Tools

Since the journey into silence is radically different from the usual religious training, metaphors and stories of journeys give prisoners a framework for their experience. If prisoners know ahead of time that part of their journey is a sense of being "lost," they will be less likely to panic and give up.

In the early days of teaching centering prayer at Folsom Prison, I struggled to put theoretical notions into practical examples from prison life that I thought would be meaningful to prisoners. I was often stumped. One day, a group member took me aside and told me, in effect, that prisoners knew prison life all too well. What they wanted were examples from everyday living "out in the world." This was the creative bridge I needed to delve into my own experiences and share these with prisoners.

> As we take up the practice of contemplation, no matter how mundane and fruitless it might seem, bit by bit our life is transformed.
> —**Gregory Mayers**, *Listen to the Desert*, p. xxiii

Similarly, if you demonstrate the importance of certain reading materials, e.g., maps for the journey, they will feel a sense of community. Prisoners, as with many of us, desperately need a sense of hope that they in fact can enter into silence and not disappear in loneliness. So it is very worthwhile at the outset to describe the pay-off of the journey—a new and true sense of self, an appreciation for one's uniqueness in the world, and an actual unmediated experience of the Divine loving you individually in your own uniqueness.

Richard Rohr's *Immortal Diamond* is of immense help here, with insights and quotes that prisoners get on the first bounce. Gregory Mayers's *Listen to the Desert* is also a great source for ideas. It may be a bit too soon to give beginners these books. It depends upon how much meditation they've done.

A Slow Pace

———

At the start, it can feel like you have so much to cover to get prisoners into centering prayer that there is a subtle need to push the pace. The opposite is the case. The more slowly you go with just a few concepts, and the sooner you give them the opportunity to do centering prayer, the more quickly they'll come to be attracted to periods of silence. Prisoners actually need very little instruction to get them into silent prayer.

> Centering prayer is not about accessing sublime states of consciousness or having mystical experiences. The fruits of this prayer are first seen in daily life.
> —**Cynthia Bourgeault**, *Centering Prayer and Inner Awakening*, p. 30

The first meeting can be that time to start the prayer. Prisoners need to know that they will not be shutting off their minds, only distracting them with a sacred word. For me, that's the place to start. I usually say something like: "The biggest misconception for beginners, and the greatest cause of discouragement, is the expectation and belief that you can shut off your mind. Never happens, even after years of meditation. It may look like this guy is off in the 'great beyond' because he is sitting perfectly still, but if I'm any example I can tell you that after 20 years of doing centering prayer, I still use my sacred word all the time."

This disclaimer is of incalculable value. It needs to be reiterated all the time for the beginner. The same caveat is necessary for evaluating the Silence afterward. Chapter Three of Cynthia Bourgeault's *Centering Prayer and Inner Awakening* is terrific on this point.

Unconscious Images of God

Prisoners get right away that there is something substantially different about centering prayer—different from nearly all other religious practices. They feel immediately the movement away from their comfort zone. Because the experience originates in Silence, our ordinary skills of critiquing are sidelined. In other words, long-held "beliefs" about the way things are, or the way we believe certain central dogmas of our religious upbringing, are subtly called into question. This shift starts with recognizing that our usual defense mechanisms are just that: defenses we use to protect our deeper selves. After a period of time, this recognition moves into a more challenging discovery that many of our foundational beliefs about the way God deals with us are open to reevaluation.

If you ask a prisoner for a definition of *God*, you'll hear the things we are all taught: all-powerful, all-loving, all-knowing, merciful, compassionate, etc., the "old man with the white beard, with the clipboard." What you won't hear about are the *actual* God images that reside in our unconscious. These are the images of God our experience has drilled into us. You won't hear about these because most of us are unaware that these images, repressed into our unconscious, are the actual images that are operative for us, e.g., God as the stern parental disciplinarian ("God is watching you"), or the judge or teacher, invested with societal authority ("You'll never amount to anything").

This reassessment of God images is an unmistakable, subtle consequence of a contemplative prayer practice. In *Finding God Within*, the awakening of our *operative* images of the Divine is crystallized in the notions of the Outside God and God Within. This changeover is the essence of the book. One of the anomalies of working with prisoners is that many come from a strict Christian upbringing—strict in the sense of an austere *understanding* of who God is and how God works in the world. Thomas Keating uses the terms *Outside God* and *Inside God* to great effect in his Spiritual Journey series, and it is particularly helpful here to overcome a critical point of experience for the prisoner.

> "Our images of God influence our religious experiences because we meet God as the one whom we image God to be. Intimacy with God is not possible when negative images and feelings make us afraid of being in God's presence."—**Wilkie Au and Noreen Cannon Au.** *God's Unconditional Love: Healing Our Shame*, pp. 45, 53.

Nearly all of us, prisoner or not, are initially saddled with the notion that we have to prove ourselves with God. For prisoners, given the events in their life, and the interpretation of these events by parental figures, the criminal justice system, and religious figures, this notion of proving ourselves to God, the need to somehow tap-dance faster so that God will notice us, is placed deep in their psyche. It's deep in mine as well, no matter the education, the "religious" experience, and the amount of contemplative prayer. I've come to believe that it is so endemic in our society and culture that we will *never* be completely free of it.

When prisoners first hear of a "prayer" practice that is Silence, it can be quite confusing. Many are used to hearing, and committed to doing, the get-on-your-knees pleading for help from the All-Powerful One. I never denigrate this type of prayer, but slowly try to undo its mooring to the core of our spiritual experience.

Many prisoners tell me that, at first, the invitation to switch from Outside God to God Within sounded like heresy. Refashioning one's image of God is enormously threatening and ultimately confronts us with the need to *choose* which model of the Divine we will follow. The first few sessions of centering prayer are not the time to force the choice—not that there is *ever* a time to *force* the choice. But the initial sessions can be gently suggestive of the need to at least recognize what our image of the God of our childhood actually is, and the God often described in our religious encounters. Richard Rohr's *The Naked Now* consistently and gently disabuses his readers with this fundamental option (see p. 37). In *Finding God Within* we wait to introduce the reader to the God Within only after covering the basics of contemplative prayer and the spiritual journey.

Fellow Travelers

The development of a contemplative mentality for prisoners is replete with confounding paradoxes that are often
confusing and not immediately capable of description. One
seeming inconsistency is that solitary prayer practices like
centering prayer also require human interaction to ground
their transformative effects. Introductory workshops of
centering prayer can often explain contemplative prayer as
"without intermediaries" or as a "direct" relationship with
the Divine. And so it is. Yet as the spiritual journey unfolds,
we understand the critical importance of relationships in
the process. It can be profoundly helpful for a prisoner
to hear that another person in the group is experiencing
greater, not lesser, anxiety with their practice. Implicitly,
group members witness their discomfort and recognize
themselves in the revelations of other group members.

> Centering Prayer will reduce anxiety perhaps for the
> first three months. But once the unconscious starts to
> unload, it will give you more anxiety than you ever
> had in your life.—**Thomas Keating**, *Intimacy with God*,
> p. 115

In my experience, this supportive group dynamic is by far the best and most direct way to illustrate the turbo-charged power of a contemplative practice. In other words, by prisoners sharing their inner experience in the group, we learn that contemplation is not the royal road to bliss, as it sometimes is mistakenly advertised as, but the experiential *via crucis* of our spiritual journey. *Silence* is key here. If the discussion time is conducted after a period of centering prayer, the group is ready to hold still and be present *in silence* to the revealing of the sufferings of a group member.

A Hedge on Discouragement

When I have only a few minutes to explain centering prayer and group meetings to a newcomer, and he or she hasn't received any materials or explanations, I concentrate on two points. The first is to *give up the notion that you can clear your mind*. Usually, a prisoner comes into a meeting for the first time because another prisoner tells him or her that centering prayer is a good experience. As they sit in a group of meditators, it's easy for them to have the mistaken notion that these practitioners' minds are empty, hence the look of peacefulness. By telling the newcomer that this isn't so, you relieve him of his initial discouragement and his feeling deficient with the "monkey-mind" experience.

It's not about an empty mind, but rather about not paying attention to their thoughts. Prisoners get right away what is meant by this example: You're in your cell watching TV and someone comes to your door. When you switch your attention to the person at the door you no longer "hear" the TV. The TV sound hasn't been lowered, but your "attention" to the sound has now been transferred to the person at your door. The same is true with "thoughts" during meditation. We never really get rid of them; we just learn not to pay any attention to them. Now, prisoners are ready to hear about the sacred word as the technique for not paying attention to their constant streaming of thoughts.

The second point of emphasis, and this applies throughout the beginning process, is that the newcomer must be *explicitly* told that the subtleties of discouragement are the real killers of the new prayer practice. Their discouragement will not be recognized as such. It will come up with thoughts like, *I'm really not cut out for sitting still, never can . . .* or *These guys are way ahead of me*, or *I'll never be able to share like this in a group of prisoners*. The constant reiteration of Thomas Keating is, "You cannot do this prayer practice wrong. The only way is by not doing it." This is *the* mantra for newcomers: they can't hear it enough. In fact, it's often used by other group members when one starts with the phrase, "The only way to do this prayer wrong. . . ."

Of course, it's critically important to connect privately with the newcomer after the meeting. You establish a primary relationship with him or her: i.e., they know you care about their experience, and it gives them an opportunity for feedback.

"I Can't Teach the Spiritual Journey"

It's one thing to teach the rudiments of centering prayer; it's a completely different thing to bravely initiate discussions about the spiritual journey. For many potential volunteers, simply the notion of getting into discussions of the spiritual journey is beyond their sense of competency. It's an intimidating prospect. Let's face it—many of us have watched Fr. Keating's Spiritual Journey Series with captivated attention. We couldn't possibly replicate that.

But there is an important distinction to recognize at the outset: *We don't have to teach it the way Fr. Keating teaches it!* The spiritual journey starts with *our* spiritual journey. We are the persons of interest. It is *our* discoveries that are relevant, not the entirety of the Christian mystical tradition. We are the true experts of our personal experience. We pick and choose more recognized "experts" for how they describe our own personal experience. These are the "teachers." Their words do the heavy lifting. They carry the weight of explaining the "mystical tradition."

Once we can hold onto this understanding, the process becomes a question of finding the best method to distill these experts' spiritual genius for our groups. Instead of *This is what I believe about this topic on the spiritual journey*, it becomes *This is what this expert says about her prayer experience. Does it make any sense to you? How does this fit with your prayer experience? What can we learn from her?* This alteration takes the pressure off us.

The change also provides an instructional method for teaching contemplative prayer in prison. Find your "expert" and share your discovery with your group. The topics will flow when you connect your own inner journey with that of your group.

Practical Realities of Going into a Prison

It's often hard to get into a prison to start a group, particularly to start what is for many an esoteric group to "meditate." From a volunteer's perspective, getting into a prison is nearly impossible unless one can find a connection with the prison chaplain. These men and women are often overworked, hard to reach, and unfamiliar with contemplative prayer.

If you are dealing with the Protestant chaplain, many stereotypes can come into play. Usually, the evangelical/fundamentalist Christian denominations are under the jurisdiction of this chaplain. Sometimes these chaplains, who are unfamiliar with the mystical contemplative tradition, confuse contemplative prayer with Buddhist "Mindfulness" meditation. Others believe that "silent meditation" is literally the "work of the devil," and will not give you the opportunity to start a group. They'll be respectful, but they will not be responsive.

Sometimes, Catholic chaplains are no different. Although often well-intentioned, many of them feel overworked and unsupported. Frequently, they are not included in the usual activities of their diocese. They function as some type of missionary outpost, remote from the bishop, and disconnected from the resources of the diocese, i.e., financial support. In this respect, they can appear unaccountable to the usual promptings of the diocese. A cold call to the Catholic chaplain in a prison can be an exercise in discouragement. Don't take this personally.

What is needed here is some personal connection to the chaplain so that he or she will understand what you are trying to start. In many dioceses, there is a designated coordinator of prison and jail chaplains. Their titles may include Director of Restorative Justice, or Social Justice Coordinator, or Director of Detention Ministry. Their responsibility is to coordinate and supervise the prison and jail chaplains in the diocese. If the diocesan director suggests to the chaplain a centering prayer program, with a volunteer ready and willing to come into the prison, you have a much greater possibility of establishing a program. If you can't find this director, usually any diocesan official can point them out. In larger dioceses, this person can be difficult to reach as well. Your networking ingenuity is essential.

Persuading prison officials can sometimes be equally daunting. Each prison has an official designated for the coordination of self-help programs. In California they are called Community Resources Managers (CRM). These officials will organize, and sometimes recruit, volunteers from the community to come into the prison for AA, NA, anger-management programs, and the like. They too, many times, feel overworked and pressed by various outside groups. Their affirmative response is necessary to let you into the prison in the first place.

If the prison chaplain and the CRM have a close working relationship, they will facilitate your clearance to get into a prison. There is an advantage in working with the Catholic chaplain to gain approval from the CRM. The advantage derives from the fact that all Catholic chaplains must have the local bishop's approval to function in the prison. This usually means that the CRM has an existing relationship with someone in the diocese. It can be most helpful for you to explain to that diocesan person, usually the Director of Restorative Justice, your wish to start a centering prayer practice.

Finally, I wish you well in following your draw into the spirituality of the incarcerated.

Part 3

Testimonies of Prisoners

Folsom State Prison

It is well worth the effort for volunteers to experience centering prayer with prisoners. We can share the loss of everything and the desire for spirituality.—**Forster Johnson**

In a centering prayer circle, each person can be who they are. As a volunteer or chaplain you must be strong enough to deal with your own pain as you are exposed to so much pain. You will see how universal this work is.—**Lawrence Hamilton**

When I started participating in a centering prayer group in prison, I was comfortable presenting the introductory workshop. I knew what to say and how to say it. But it was rote, largely in my head, and surrounded with somewhat pietistic language. I had to go back to basics, into my heart, and wrestle in the agony and ecstasy of my relationship with God. Now, when I go into a prison group I ask: *Is it true for me? Is it real?*—**Susan Turpin**, Volunteer

Ask yourself: How do you view anyone who has committed a crime? Would you take the time to seek out their reason for a crime?—**David Bonner**

You must not feel pressure to bestow profound wisdom. What you say is not as important as just being present. **—Paul Dietering**

Know that prisoners in centering prayer circles have made a conscious free choice to embark on a spiritual journey of a lifetime.**—Schacobie Manning**

Listen to comments. As in most relationships, many prisoners just want to be heard. If you truly care, then it is always worth your effort as you will affect people's lives in a positive way.**—Name withheld**

We will welcome a volunteer who is willing to come inside to help us on our spiritual journey to learn more about the "Inside God."**—Aaron Jones**

The experience of interacting with prisoners is mutually rewarding so long as the volunteer's effort is genuine and coming from non-judgmental spirituality.**—Claudio Arena**

Many, if not all, of those incarcerated have been beaten down and dehumanized by their imprisonment. Human-to-human communion, like centering prayer and sharing, is the elixir that facilitates the rediscovery of one's humanity. All sides benefit, regardless of status.**—Joshua Gilmore**

Volunteers bring strength and hope to us who have been stripped from the outside world. So bring your true self, and try to leave your false self at the gate. Welcome!**—Jeff Clay**

Do not fear us. The fear will cause you to pull away. If you withdraw, we will not receive what we need from you, the understanding that we are just like you. When you come, the madness of prison life stops.—**Artis Knox**

Centering prayer groups are not the place for "preaching" and trying to "convert" what some may perceive as the "great unwashed." Centering prayer is the most powerful tool to free us, inmate or "freeperson," from the prison of our own unconscious.—**Harvey Jacobs**

Through Prison Contemplative Fellowship I've learned to understand the distorted belief of how I viewed myself and detach from that old belief.—**Steve Sidharta**

Just as martial arts are used for self-defense and discipline, centering prayer and meditation are like that. Meditation calms the mind when your outside world is in chaos. Meditation also defends the actions you want to take when you don't need to take them. It is well worth the effort to have this practice in my life; in some way it helps cleanse my heart and mind.—**Liu**

Centering prayer and fellowship give me the ability to be the quiet, peaceful, and helpful man I want to be. It allows me to give some small amount of kindness back to another.—**William Hays**

Folsom Women's Prison

I encourage anyone who has been called as a volunteer or a chaplain to be of service to come and sit in silence and be with God. Not only would your life change but you could help change the lives of those in prison. Centering prayer has given me an experience of freedom. I will forever be changed. I have found who I am and am so blessed to have this group available to me. I love the group and want to say thank you to God for the volunteers and centering prayer.—**Nassima Boulazreg**

I want to say to volunteers that we need you. Life in prison is very hard; actually it can be extremely hard. Having compassionate people around us gives us hope. Thank you.—**Name withheld**

The open environment to all religious beliefs helps me feel comfortable. As I deepen my meditation practice, I often find the shared insights touch everyone.—**Meghan Stewart**

California Health Care Facility

We encourage you to join us. Your efforts with us are worthwhile. We would like you to take some of our wisdom of God into your communities to strengthen other concepts of contemplative prayer.—**Lawrence Davis III**

Hold on! You're going on a ride and you will not want to get off. You will find peace and joy in yourself and inside of someone incarcerated that you didn't think possible.
—Michael Fennell

Had it not been for volunteers there would not have been any rehabilitation process in my life. I've learned to be a human being with value even after I was thrown away as garbage.—**Ed Bowman**

Building a bond of trust with volunteers allows us to express our hidden feelings. We understand your fear when you first come into a prison. We're not bad people. No different from the people next door to you. We all make mistakes. Inmates are good judges of people and know when you're not real with us. They don't like a liar or fake person. Don't let the silence scare you. It's an experience that will fill your life with warmth and Godly love as you recognize your true self.
—Harold Lawley Sr.

Deuel Vocational Institute

Your efforts with us strengthen our ability to control our emotions and become better persons.—**Antonio Conde**

Let volunteers know that they need not worry about what they share. We do not judge nor debate. Listening and sharing has helped me find inner peace without shame. —**Louie**

The gratitude that many of us feel toward those volunteers who week-in and week-out sacrifice their time, resources, and energy toward helping us is a deep and genuine feeling. We understand that without you our journey toward enlightenment and spirituality are not possible. . . . These blessings are available to all who are a part of Prison Contemplative Fellowship. That's why we return every week.—**George Ferguson**

As a man who has been incarcerated for nearly 24 years, I can say that centering prayer has allowed me to build a closer relationship with God in a setting of peace, trust, support, and fellowship among my fellow inmates. There is a sense of friendship and community among this centering prayer group of men from different backgrounds and

ethnicities. This group allows us to be adult men without being concerned with what others may think or say.
—**Mark B.**

As a volunteer I find I am learning with the prisoners. As I share my ups and downs of the journey, I am learning about myself and I see how others can relate to my experiences. The experience of Divine Therapy is life-changing. When I first met the men, they were prisoners. Then I saw them as hurting human beings seeking God and peace. Now I see and think of them as friends.
—**Amelia Stovall**, Volunteer

We need people from outside the prison to know that many of us have made bad choices but have changed. We have the same ideals as they do. We need to be accepted. Volunteers need to see this. We have no voice. We can only prove our changed point of view if we are seen.
—**No name given**

I have found no better way to connect and improve my conscious contact with God than through centering prayer. You may feel alone, but you're a part of a group who draws strength from each other.—**Anonymous**

We prisoners are God's creation. We know that God is love. Come walk with us on our journey. Together, we can change for the better and make our world a good place.
—**Jose Moreno**

Contemplative prayer has helped me find God Within, if I just sit in quiet and listen. It's worth the effort.
—**Javier Arzaga**

Both prisoners and volunteers profit much. We learn from each other and perpetuate the positive energy.
—**Calvin Johnson**

The volunteers are priceless. They are proof that I am worth redeeming. I lost my way and they have shown me that the trail was always there for me. Through them, God showed me I was worth saving.—**Ronald Willey**

Suggestions for Further Reading and Resources

These are the books I returned to, time and again, to help me understand, then explain, important notions regarding contemplation and the spiritual journey.

Au, Wilkie, and Noreen Cannon Au. *God's Unconditional Love: Healing Our Shame*. Mahwah, N.J.: Paulist Press, pp. 35–58

Bourgeault, Cynthia. *Centering Prayer and Inner Awakening*. Cambridge: Cowley Publications, 2004

Keating, Thomas. *Intimacy with God*. New York: Crossroad, 2000

____. *Invitation to Love*. New York: Continuum, 2004

May, Gerald. *Will and Spirit*. San Francisco: Harper, 1982

Rohr, Richard. *Breathing under Water: Spirituality and the Twelve Steps*. Cincinnati: St. Anthony Messenger, 2011

____. *Immortal Diamond: The Search For the True Self*. San Francisco: Jossey–Bass, 2013

____. *The Naked Now: Learning to See as the Mystics See*. New York: Crossroad, 2009

Please see our website, USPCF.org, for an extended list of readings for specific topics. The list also contains quotations that may be useful to reproduce as a handout for *lectio divina.*

Resources

Center for Action and Contemplation: P.O. Box 12464, Albuquerque, NM 87195-2464 cac.org

Contemplative Outreach, 10 Park Place, Second Floor Suite B., Butler, NJ 07405, www.contemplativeoutreach.org

Human Kindness Foundation, P.O. Box 61619, Durham, NC 27715, www.humankindness.org

Prison Contemplative Fellowship, P.O. Box 1086, Folsom, CA 95763-1086, USPCF.org

Acknowledgments

Going Inside is the product of comments and suggestions from prisoners, volunteers, family, and friends. The prisoners are identified in the book and illustrate the spectrum of insight that forms the foundation of the work. They ground the book in the reality of life in prison.

Volunteers who go into prisons with me and some who don't provided much appreciated observations and clarifications. In particular, Tim O'Connell, Ellie Shea, Chuck McIntyre, Susan and Paul Turpin, Janice Boyd, and Al Franklin kept me focused and energized in the project. Martin Rowe of Lantern enhanced the book in numerous ways.

Two editors—one professional, the other personal— offered vital perspectives: Marilyn Chandler McEntyre, herself an author of a number of remarkable spiritual books, would ask: *Is this really what you want to say?* The other, my wife, Cherla Leonardini, would ask: *Do you really believe this?* Their diligent perspectives gave me the confidence to continue. Thank you.

About the Author

Ray Leonardini is a former lawyer who practiced government and nonprofit law for nearly thirty years. After his retirement, he turned toward his foremost area of interest: the Christian contemplative tradition. For the last nine years, as a volunteer chaplain, he has led meditation groups and taught contemplative prayer and the spiritual journey at Folsom State Prison in California. He is also the Director of the Prison Contemplative Fellowship, an association of current and former prison inmates, chaplains, and volunteers committed to reaching out to prisoners and their families on their travels along the spiritual path.

Also by Lantern Books

The Thomas Keating Reader
Selected Writings from the Contemplative Outreach Newsletter

The Transformation of Suffering
*Reflections on September 11
and the Wedding Feast in Cana Galilee*

About the Publisher

LANTERN BOOKS was founded in 1999 on the principle of living with a greater depth and commitment to the preservation of the natural world. In addition to publishing books on animal advocacy, vegetarianism, religion, and environmentalism, Lantern is dedicated to printing books in the U.S. on recycled paper and saving resources in day-to-day operations. Lantern is honored to be a recipient of the highest standard in environmentally responsible publishing from the Green Press Initiative.

LANTERNBOOKS.COM